Mexico is my country

In this book 26 people from all over Mexico tell you what their life is like—life in the cities and villages, along the coast, and in the mountains.

MEXICO
is my country

Bernice and Cliff Moon

Wayland

My Country

America is my country
Argentina is my country
Australia is my country
Brazil is my country
Britain is my country
Canada is my country
China is my country
Denmark is my country
France is my country
Greece is my country
India is my country
Israel is my country
Italy is my country
Japan is my country
Kenya is my country
Mexico is my country
New Zealand is my country
Pakistan is my country
Spain is my country
The European U.S.S.R. is my country
West Germany is my country

This book is based on We live in Mexico, *in Wayland's 'Living Here' series, by Carlos Somonte.*

First published in 1986 by
Wayland (Publishers) Ltd
61 Western Road, Hove
East Sussex BN3 1JD, England

© Copyright 1986 Wayland (Publishers) Ltd

British Library Cataloguing in Publication Data

Moon, Bernice
   Mexico is my country.—(My country)
   1. Mexico—Social life and customs—Case studies—
   —Juvenile literature
   I. Title II. Moon, Cliff III. Series
   972.08′34′0926   F1210

ISBN 0-85078-659-2

Phototypeset by Latimer Trend & Company Ltd, Plymouth
Printed in Italy by G. Canale & C.S.p.A., Turin
Bound in the UK at The Bath Press, Avon

Contents

Luis, *schoolboy* 6
Eduardo, *cowboy* 8
Juan, *fisherman* 10
Valentin, *train driver* 12
Celestino, *weaver* 14
Rosalba, *archaeologist* 16
Ignacio, *high diver* 18
Agripina, *stall holder* 20
Alvaro, *pilot* 22
Kin, *Indian* 24
Clara, *dolphin trainer* 26
Gabriel, *cameraman* 28
Javier, *oil-rig worker* 30
Don, *cactus grower* 32
Filiberto, *car mechanic* 34
Jacinta, *street actor* 36
Camilo, *Indian* 38
Luis, *baseball player* 40
Rosa, *teacher* 42
Pedro, *sells spices* 44
Horacio, *drives a rock-lifter* 46
Amelia, *musician* 48
Enrique, *customs officer* 50
Fernando, *biologist* 52
Maria, *police student* 54
Leobardo, *photographer* 56
Facts 58
Index 60

My name is Luis. I'm a schoolboy

I live in a small
fishing village called
Paraiso Escondido
on the west coast
of Mexico.
Every day I walk 3 km
(2 miles) to school, but
first I have to cross
a river in my boat.
I leave home at 7 a.m.
but school ends at 2 p.m.
so I get home early.

My boat is called a *cayuco* and I use it
when I go fishing in the river.

My father is a fisherman and he goes out
into the Pacific Ocean in his motor boat.
Sometimes he catches a really big fish like a shark or a barracuda.
I usually catch catfish and I know how to trap crabs
with small traps called *jaiberos*.
Sometimes I catch shrimps with my net and my mother
makes tasty soups with them.

I go to a primary school which is for children aged 6 to 12 years.
After that I shall go to a secondary school for three years,
then to a high school and perhaps college or university.

I am Eduardo.
I'm a cowboy.

In Mexico a lasso is called a *reata*.
I use my *reata* to lasso cattle and horses but sometimes I do tricks to amuse my children.

Foals are difficult to catch without a *reata*.

I work on a ranch in the northern State of Sonora.
Sonora is known as a cattle rearing area.
The climate here is very hot and dry.
Summer is our wettest season, but even then we don't get much rain.
I ride my horse all day in the hot sun,
looking after 800 head of cattle and checking fences.
I always carry wire, nails and a hammer with me
for mending broken fences.
By 1 p.m. the temperature has risen to about 36°C (97°F)
and that's when the rattlesnakes come out to bask on
the warm rocks.
I only kill them if they get too close to the
ranch buildings, because a rattlesnake bite can kill you.

I'm called Juan.
I'm a fisherman.

I live with my wife on the shore of Lake Pátzcuaro
in the State of Michoacán.
The Michoacán lakes are famous for their tasty white fish.

My wife often helps me to check our fishing net and
she sells all the fish I catch.

Lake Pátzcuara is
very beautiful and
many people come here
for their holidays.
There are green hills
and mountains near
the shore.
Tourists like to buy
my fresh white fish.

I drop my net into
the lake in the evening
and leave it overnight.
Now it is morning
and I am pulling it in
to see what I have caught.

Before I start fishing, I have to cut a channel
through the water plants that grow in the lake.
I do this from my boat using a sharp hook on a long pole.
I drop my net into the channel and it forms a
sort of curtain which the fish swim into.

I am Valentin and I am a train driver.

If you ever travel on my train you will see wonderful scenery.
We start in Ojinaga, which is on the border with the USA.
From Ojinaga we go across the hot dry plains to Chihuahua.
Then the train starts its climb into the forests
of the Sierra Madre Occidental.
This is a range of mountains which runs down eastern Mexico.
The views are breathtaking, especially when we pass through
an area called the Tarahumaran Sierra.
Here you can see deep canyons cut into the rocks
by mountain torrents.
The train twists and turns over 36 bridges and
through 86 tunnels on its journey.
It takes nearly a day to reach Topolobampo on the Pacific coast,
where our journey of 920 kilometres (572 miles) ends.

Sometimes the hills in the Sierra Madre are so steep we can only travel at 10 km/h (6 m.p.h.)

I enjoy looking at the scenery from the cab of my train.

13

I am Celestino.
I'm a weaver.

I weave carpets on
wooden looms like these.
We work them with
our hands and feet.
The carpets are
made from wool.

My wool is coloured with dyes which I make myself
from fruit, vegetables and insects.
I use pomegranates, tomatoes, watermelons and leaves
to make pink and red, and I also use the cochineal beetle
to make a very bright red.
Nuts are useful for making a brown dye.

I live with my family in the south of Mexico
at Teotitlán Del Valle in the State of Oaxaca.
Only 6,000 people live in the town and
nearly all of us make hand-woven cloth.
My father taught me how to weave when I was eleven
and now I am teaching my son, José.

José and I have just finished this carpet.
The colours and patterns are taken from old Indian designs.

I am Rosalba and I am an archaeologist.

At Palenque, in the far south of Mexico,
there are some very old and beautiful Mayan temples.
I work on the repair and preservation of these temples.

Altogether there are 30 of us working here. Wind and tropical rain have damaged the temples and there is a lot of rebuilding to do.

This is one of the old Mayan temples at Palenque.

The temples are about 1,000 years old and they were built by the Indians who lived in Mexico from AD 300 to AD 900. The Mayans knew a great deal about mathematics and astronomy. Their calculations were very accurate and they knew exactly when there would be an eclipse of the sun.

I'm called Ignacio and I am a high diver.

I live and work in Acapulco, which is one of the world's most famous holiday resorts.
Tourists come to Acapulco to see its beautiful beaches and swim in its warm, blue water.
Some come to see the famous *La Quebrada* high divers.

Here I am with four other *La Quebrada* high divers.

We dive 35 metres (115 feet)
from the cliff into
only 4 metres (13 feet)
of water.

Before I make my high dive,
I have to climb the cliff
as there aren't any steps.
I say a quick prayer
and then I dive.
It feels as though
I am flying.
Now that I'm 34,
I'm not as fit as
I used to be, but
I practise every day
and I've won the world
high-dive championship
three times.

I am Agripina and I am a stall holder.

I have had a craft stall in the huge Libertad market at Guadalajara ever since it opened 22 years ago. Everything on my stall has been made by craftsmen and women from all over Mexico.
I sell hand-painted pottery, wooden carvings, stone tools, paintings and toys.
At the market there are lots of fruit and vegetable stalls which sell melons, tomatoes, strawberries, peppers and chillies. There are also stalls which sell herbs and spices for cooking and medicines.
In the summer, I sell a lot of pottery jars and beakers because the pottery helps to keep the water cool and fresh. December is the busiest month of the year at the market as this is when everyone is looking for Christmas presents.

I have just sold some colourful beakers to a tourist.
My daughter often helps me during the school holidays.
We open the stall at 10 a.m. and close at 7 p.m.

This is just one small part of the Libertad market.

My name is Alvaro. I'm a pilot.

There are more than 160 airline companies in Mexico.
Planes fly between all the main towns and cities.

Air travel is important in a country as large as Mexico. For example, if you travel from Mexico City to Mérida by car it will take a day or more, but if you fly it only takes one and a half hours.
We also have airstrips in remote mountain areas. Archaeologists who work on the Mayan temples are flown to Chiapas State in light aircraft.

22

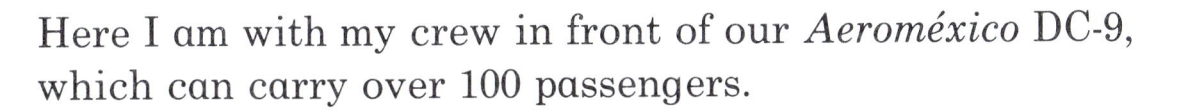

Here I am with my crew in front of our *Aeroméxico* DC-9, which can carry over 100 passengers.

We get used to flying through all kinds of weather. When it is very dry we may have to fly through dust storms, and in the rainy season between July and September we can get torrential rain storms.

I'm called Kin
I'm an Indian.

I live with my wife and daughter in the jungles of the State of Chiapas in the south-east of Mexico. We are members of the Lacandon tribe, which is descended from the Maya.
Here I am with my family and relations.

I spend some of my time making bows and arrows
which I sell to tourists.

Indians have lived in the State of Chiapas for
hundreds of years. We find everything we need in the jungle.
Our homes are made from wood and clay.
There is water for drinking and plenty of fresh fruit
and meat to eat.
We gather plants which make us better when we are ill.

I use my bow and arrows to hunt for animals.
The flights on my arrows are made from parrot feathers.
I know which animals are safe and which are dangerous.
Deer, birds and monkeys do not harm us, but
we have to watch out for poisonous spiders and
fierce jungle cats which attack cattle and children.
Some of the snakes are 8 metres (26 feet) long and
they can swallow a deer whole.

My name is Clara and I'm a dolphin trainer.

Dolphins are clever animals and it is easy to train them to do tricks.
I train five dolphins.
We put on three shows during the week and four over the weekend.
We are based next to an amusement park, so most of the people who come to our shows are children.

Every time my dolphins perform well I blow my whistle
and give them some fish.
My dolphins perform in Mexico City, the capital of Mexico.
I like to spend my spare time reading about the history of
Mexico City. It is built on the site of the first capital city
of Mexico, called Tenochtitlán, which was a huge place
with temples, pyramids, markets, workshops and
canals like those at Venice in Italy.
But in 1521, Cortés and his army of Spanish soldiers
attacked the city and completely destroyed it.
A few years later the Spanish built Mexico City
on the ruins of Tenochtitlán.

My name is Gabriel. I'm a cameraman.

American producers often come to Mexico to film Westerns
and they usually employ Mexican film crews.
I have filmed nearly 200 movies and at the moment
I am working on a film called *Under the Volcano*,
which is about Mexico in the 1930s.
We are filming in the State of Morelos, which is
a beautiful area south of Mexico City
with spring-like weather all the year round.
Near to where we are filming, there are two volcanoes:
Popocatépetl ('The Smoking Mountain') and
Ixtaccíhuatl ('The Sleeping Woman').
An old Indian story says that these volcanoes were once
a prince and princess who were not allowed to marry, and
because of this the princess died of a broken heart.
When Popocatépetl rumbles, the Indians say
that it is the prince crying for his dead sweetheart.

The peak of Popocatépetl is covered with snow.

This is a film set for *Under the Volcano* which stars Albert Finney and Jacqueline Bisset.

29

I am Javier and I am an oil-rig worker.

I work for the state petrol company called Pemex. We are drilling for oil near Villahermosa. We think the oil is 6,000 metres (19,700 feet) underground.
My job is to test soil samples which tell us how close we are getting to the oil.

Our rig is on dry land in a tropical forest area, but
Pemex has other oil rigs in the shallow waters
around the Gulf of Mexico.
Oil is an important fuel in Mexico because
it is used to provide energy for our factories and homes.
About 90 per cent of the nation's energy comes from oil.
A lot of oil is sold to other countries too, and
this brings foreign money into Mexico.
Every day Mexico produces nearly 3 million barrels
of crude oil and over 4 million cubic feet of natural gas.

This is the oil rig where I'm testing soil samples.

My name is Don and I am a cactus grower.

The juice from the type of cactus that I grow can be made into an alcoholic drink called tequila.

Today my workers are clearing weeds around the cactus plants.

I grow more than 780,000 cactus plants
on my dry, sandy plantations.

Our plants grow for eight to ten years
before they are ready for tapping the juice.
We clear weeds away every three months and
the soil is fertilized once a year.
When the cacti have been growing for three years,
I trim the points of the leaves so that they will grow larger.

Drinks made from cactus juice are popular all over Mexico
and there are many cactus farms in hot, dry areas.
We make drinks called *pulque* and *mescal* from cactus.
We drink tequila with salt and freshly-squeezed lemon juice.
We grow a lot of fruit in Mexico, and freshly-squeezed juices
can be bought in towns and villages everywhere.

I am Filiberto and I'm a car mechanic.

I work for the Mexican Tourist Board.
Every week I travel up to 350 kilometres
(217 miles) answering calls for help from tourists
whose cars have broken down.
I patrol the state highway in the State of Vera Cruz.

We use green breakdown vans which are controlled by radio. People call us the 'Green Angels'.

My van is fitted with everything I need to repair cars.
Most breakdowns are caused by broken fan belts, flat batteries,
dirty spark plugs or empty fuel tanks.
I have to carry a fire extinguisher, but
I prefer to put out fires with Coca-Cola!
I carry three large bottles of Coca-Cola and
when there's a fire I give the bottles a really good shake
to build up pressure, and then I spray the fire with it.

With 212,500 kilometres (132,000 miles) of roads and
over 3,700,000 cars in Mexico, we are always busy.

I am Jacinta.
I'm a street actor.

I really enjoy doing mime, pantomimes and puppet shows on street corners, in underground stations and in parks. I have acted in Veracruz, Oaxaca, Guadalajara and Mexico City, and at Covent Garden in London and the Pompidou Centre in Paris.

I don't earn enough money from street acting, so I model for artists and make pottery which I sell.

Diego and I are miming in the street.
All kinds of people stop to watch us.

I have always loved colour and art.
In Mexico we have many wonderful paintings
on the fronts of buildings and on walls.
Costumes worn at festivals are full of colour too,
especially those worn for the famous Dance of the Quetzal.
The quetzal is a bird that lives in the jungles of the south.
It has brilliant green, red and white feathers and a crest.
The dancers copy the bird by wearing a beautiful head-dress
like the huge open fan of a peacock.

My name is Camilo. I'm an Indian.

I live in the Urique Canyon which is one of the deep canyons of the Tarahumaran Sierra in northern Mexico.
The canyons are covered by forests and we make our cabins from logs and stones.
I grow my own vegetables and fruit, and
I also have eight goats and three chickens
which provide me with milk and eggs.

The Tarahumaran Sierra is a wild place but more than 50,000 Indians live here.

I know how to hunt deer by tracking them
for hours or even days.
When the winter snows arrive I take my family
lower down the canyon.
We walk for up to six hours at a time along small trails
that wind their way down to the warmer lowlands.

I love to sit on a high rock where I can see
a long way across the Tarahumaran Sierra.

▼

My name is Luis and I am a baseball player.

I love baseball.
We call it the 'King of Sports'.
Baseball is played all over Mexico, but it is most popular along the coast of the Gulf of Mexico.

I often take my son to the practice sessions which we have at least twice a week.
My team has won the local championships for two years now and we hope to play against teams from other countries.

During the week, I work as a welder in a factory
which repairs trucks and earth-moving machinery.

Mexicans love to take part in sport.
We play the fastest ball game in the world, called *jai alai*.
Football is very popular and so is boxing.
Then there is the *charreada* which is like a rodeo.
Horsemen dressed in colourful costumes and huge sombreros
ride skilfully after young bulls and wild horses to lasso them.

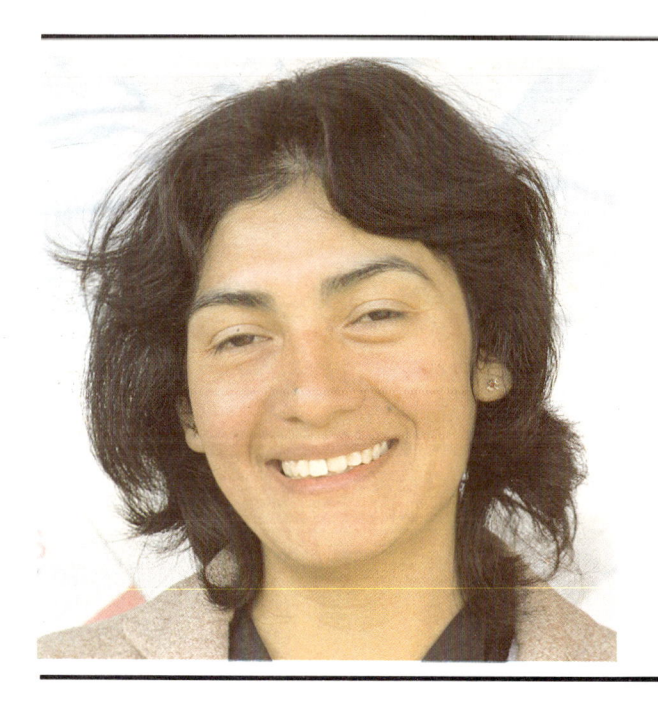

My name is Rosa
I'm a teacher.

I am a primary school teacher in a small town in the State of Tlaxcala near Mexico City.

Most of my class of 8-year-old children live on farms in the surrounding countryside.

Here I am with my class on the school's basketball court.

We start school at 8 a.m. and finish at 12.30 p.m.
Then there's one hour for lunch, when most of my children eat packed lunches which they have brought from home.
We have two 10-minute breaks during the morning.
After school, many of the children spend the afternoon helping their parents on the farm.

Children come to our school when they are 6 and leave when they are 12.
My class has different teachers for P.E. and music, but I teach them everything else from Spanish to maths.

I am Pedro and I sell spices.

I run the largest spice shop in Oaxaca City.
I sell more than 30 different kinds of chilli pepper
as well as many other kinds of hot spices.
Chillies are small pods which give food a hot taste.
They can be yellow, green or red.

This is my brother.
He is cleaning chillies
and putting them
into a basket
ready to sell
in my shop.

Mexicans eat a lot of sweet corn and beans.
They also make a kind of pancake called a *tortilla*
with maize or wheat flour.
You can find a shop selling *tortillas* on almost every
street corner. *Tacos* and *tamales* are other types of flour
pancakes and, like *tortillas*, they can be filled with chicken,
grated cheese, onion, tomato sauce or chilli sauce.
Oaxaca City is well known for its *moles*.
A *mole* is a sauce made from more than 30 ingredients.

This is my shop with its baskets piled high with chillies.

45

I am Horacio and I drive a rock-lifter.

I drive the largest rock-lifter in Mexico.
It is a 70-tonne machine which can lift rocks
as heavy as 30 tonnes. At the moment
we are building a breakwater for the port of Ensenada.
I load the rocks into huge trucks
which then dump them in the sea.

The Ensenada breakwater will take more than a year to build.

I have worked at large ports like Veracruz, Tampico and Coatzacoalcos on the Gulf of Mexico and Mazatlán, and Acapulco and Salina Cruz on the Pacific Coast.

In Mexico we mine silver, mercury, cadmium, manganese and zinc which are sold to the USA, Spain, Israel, Japan, West Germany and Brazil.
All these goods are exported by sea so we need large ports.
Mexico also sells a lot of oil and this is shipped from Coatzacoalcos, Tampico and Salina Cruz.
Machinery, coffee, tomatoes, cotton and shrimps are also exported by sea.

I am Amelia.
I'm a musician.

I am very interested in the music that was played by the Indians before the Spanish came to Mexico.

I give Indian music concerts with my friends, Antonio and Germán.

I own a large collection
of Indian instruments.
I have big shells,
flutes, drums and
teponaztlis, which are
hollow logs played with
wooden sticks.
Some of these instruments
were played when a baby
was born or when someone died.
Sometimes different instruments
were used to let people
know the time, to send
messages or to warn them
that it would soon rain.

People would often dance to the music
just as they do today at a *fiesta*.
A fiesta is a holiday or carnival, usually on a saint's day.
Sometimes it lasts for a week or more.
At each fiesta there is music, dancing, a procession and
a firework display.

I am Enrique and I am a customs officer.

I work at Tijuana which is on the border between Mexico and the USA. Holidaymakers often visit Tijuana for shopping and sightseeing.

Up to 1,000 cars a minute can pass through Tijuana from the USA, and over 30 million people come through the town every year.
The border is over 2,494 kilometres (1,550 miles) long.
We cannot patrol all of it so it's quite easy for criminals to escape from one country to the other.

I first worked in the south on the Mexico–Guatemala border. I rode 45 kilometres (28 miles) on horseback every day, trying to stop the smuggling of coffee and cocoa into Mexico. But I was soon posted to Tijuana where I have had lots of adventures. Once I caught an American murderer who was trying to hide a body in Mexico.
Another time I arrested a man who was carrying 1.5 million dollars which he had stolen in a robbery in the USA.

Millions of holidaymakers cross the Mexican border each year.

I am Fernando.
I'm a biologist.

A biologist is a person who studies animals and plants.
I am especially interested in the animal and plant life
of the sea, and I am studying turtles at the moment.
There are seven types of turtle in the sea
off the east and west coasts of Mexico.
For six months of the year I work on the beaches
near Colima and Oaxaca, where the turtles come ashore
to lay their eggs before going back into the sea.
I tag turtles while they are on the beach.
A tag is fixed on the turtle's fin, giving
the date, the name of the beach and the country
in which it has been tagged.
If the turtle is found again, we can find out how far it went.
I once found a turtle which had been tagged
off the French coast on the other side of the Atlantic.

I have to write notes on everything I find and I make a list of all the turtles I tag.

Today I am making sure that these baby turtles reach the water safely.

My name is Maria and I am a police student.

I am training at Mexico City police college.
I get up at 5 a.m., have a cold shower
and then go to an hour's P.E. class.
Breakfast is at 7 a.m. and lectures begin at 8 a.m.
We have to learn about traffic laws and also
what to do when there is an accident.

The Mexican flag is raised every day in the central square of the Mexico City police college.

After lectures I go to judo and karate classes.
I shall need to know how to defend myself,
especially in a place like Mexico City.
About 14 million people live in Mexico City.
There are many wide roads and over 2 million cars
are driven in the city every day.

The police college supplies our uniforms and also
pays us a monthly wage of 28,000 pesos (£108).

I am Leobardo and I am a photographer.

I work at the shrine of the Virgin of Guadalupe, in the La Villa area of Mexico City.

People like to have their pictures taken in front of these religious scenes.

People come to the holy shrine from all over Mexico.
These men have cycled a long way to get here.

But why was the shrine built?
People say that in 1531 the Virgin Mary came to see
a young Indian boy called Juan Diego.
She asked him to build a church for her.
She told Juan to go up into the hills and
pick all the roses he could find there.
It was during the dry, winter season when there were no roses,
but Juan found the most beautiful roses he'd ever seen.
He picked them and put them into his large cotton shirt.
When he got back to the town Juan told the priests
what had happened, and when he took out the roses
everyone saw a picture of the Virgin Mary printed on his shirt.
Our shrine stands on the spot where Juan first saw Mary.

Facts

Capital City   The capital city of Mexico is Mexico City.

Language   Most people in Mexico speak Spanish. Five groups of Indian languages are also spoken. They are Náhuatl, Maya, Zapotec, Otomi and Mixtec.

Money   People in Mexico pay for things with *centavos* and *pesos*. There are 100 centavos in 1 peso.

People   There are 67,405,700 people in Mexico. Over one-fifth of them live in and around Mexico City. Nearly half the population is under 15 years old.

Weather   Mexico is very hot and damp. The south gets a lot of rain and it is much cooler in the mountains. It is very dry in the north and west.

Churches   Most Mexicans are Roman Catholics.

Government   Mexico is a republic with 31 states. The President is chief of state and of the government.

Houses   Too many people have moved from the
country to the cities, and there are
not enough houses for everyone.
Many live in shanty slums.

Schools   Children go to primary school
from the ages of 6 to 12 and then
they go to secondary school for three years.
After that they can go to high school
and then to college or university.

Farming   Mexican farmers grow sweet corn, beans
rice, wheat, sugar cane, coffee, cotton,
tomatoes, chillies, peppers, cacti and
many kinds of fruit.

Factories   Silver, graphite, mercury, cadmium,
manganese and zinc are mined.
Factories produce cars, cement,
clothes, paper and beer.

News   There are seven TV channels and
there is also a cable TV channel from
the USA.

Index

Acapulco 18, 19, 47
acting 36, 37

borders 12, 50, 51

cacti 32, 33, 59
cattle 8, 9
Cortés 27

dancing 37, 49

exports 31, 47

factories 31, 41, 59
farming 8, 9, 32, 33, 42, 43, 59
fiestas 49
films 28, 29
fishing 7, 10, 11
food 7, 10, 11, 14, 20, 25, 38, 39, 43, 44, 45, 47, 51, 59

government 59

holidays 11, 18, 50, 51
houses 31, 59

Indians 15, 17, 24, 25, 38, 39, 48, 49, 58

lasso 8, 9, 41
Libertad market 20, 21,

Maya 16, 17, 22, 58
Mexico City 22, 27, 28, 42, 54, 55, 56, 57, 58
money 55, 58
mountains 12, 13, 28, 29, 38, 39, 58
music 48, 49

oil 30, 31, 47

religion 56, 57, 58
roads 34, 35, 55

schools 6, 7, 42, 43, 59
snakes 9, 25
sport 40, 41, 43

television 59
tequila 32, 33
tourists 8, 21, 25, 34
turtles 52, 53

weather 9, 16, 23, 39, 58
weaving 14, 15